BRITAIN IN OLD PH   HS

HAVANT &
HAYLING ISLAND

ROBERT COOK

SUTTON PUBLISHING

Sutton Publishing Limited
Phoenix Mill · Thrupp · Stroud
Gloucestershire · GL5 2BU

First published 1996

Reprinted in 2004

Copyright © Robert Cook, 1996

Title page photograph: Havant station,
AIX loco pulling the 'Hayling Billy' train
into Havant, 3 May 1953. (B.K.B. Green)

British Library Cataloguing in Publication Data
A catalogue record for this book is available from the
British Library.

ISBN 0 7509 1317 7

Typeset in 10/12 Perpetua.
Typesetting and origination by
Sutton Publishing Limited.
Printed in Great Britain by
J.H. Haynes & Co., Ltd, Sparkford.

Langstone Mill looking more like a pagoda during repair work in the 1990s. (M. Hudson)

CONTENTS

Looking north over Havant town centre in 1963. North and South Streets make a neat right-hand boundary to the picture, divided at the crossroads by their junction with West Street, the old A27. St Faith's Church is a prominent feature in the foreground. (*Portsmouth News*)

INTRODUCTION

I first visited Havant in the summer of 1974. In those days I was an offspring of self-indulgent 1970s youth culture – some might prefer to say idealistic. My original reason for coming to the town was romantic, but in a strange contrast I ended up working in the local tax office. Hence the first great character I recall from the area was my District Tax Inspector Fred Eavis. He was a matter-of-fact man who had served in the Army and remembered the war. He chastised me for being an intellectual and said I reminded him of his University lecturer-type batman who never knew whether to press his boots or polish his trousers. I disliked Fred's humour at the time because I did not understand it. There was a mighty generation gap between us. But now, perhaps, there seems to be an even wider gap between myself and today's youth, and so I can appreciate his despair. He could not see the world from my point of view. As a wise old man told me recently, each generation has its own ideas and tolerances and one can never fully understand the other. But most of us do our best.

I struggle to understand the past and the present. How we interpret events depends very much on background and experience. But there are at least some simple facts to start with. Havant stood on a crossroads where the Roman route from old Winchester intersected the coastal road from Clausentum (Bitterne near Southampton) to Regnum (Chichester), and went on to meet the coast at Langston and then across the Wadeway to Hayling Island. In the twelfth century St Faith's Church was built at this crossroads and Christianity lent its civilizing hand.

But the reign of William the Conqueror had placed limits on this civilization and restricted freedom. Jesus's simple teachings were turned to the King's own ends. And so it was handed down through the years. Singing sweetly, local schoolchildren would have the idea reinforced: 'The rich man in his castle, the poor man at his gate, God made them high or lowly and ordered their estate. All things bright and beautiful, the Lord God made them all.' Or, as observed symbolically in a newspaper column by 'Once a week' in 1869, writing about Langstone Mill: it 'stood fast with outstretched arms . . . and blown by revolutionary winds, observed by routine duty.'

In 1842 Havant had six malt-houses and five breweries. Samuel Glynne of West Street grew barley and brewed for his pubs, the Black Dog, the George and the Bear. Beer drinking, as I know from bitter (pardon the pun) experience, is one way of deadening unpleasant experiences and is as popular as ever, though the breweries today are larger and fewer. I remember listening to 'The way we were' playing on the juke-box at the Wheelwright in 1975 and perhaps looking as if I was crying into my beer, when Mr Mancini the landlord comforted me with a similar expression and the words 'life's a sad business'. I also remember my landlady in Lymbourne Road telling me about her hard times and that I had nothing to complain about. Nothing could be as bad as the days of the workhouse, could it? Then heroes came back from Waterloo and couldn't get a drink in Portsmouth. They had to march north as far as an inn in Wait Lane End. It had no name then so they called it Heroes of Waterloo. Eventually the name became shortened to Waterloo and a hamlet grew up around it. To avoid confusion with Waterloo in Lancashire, 'ville' was subsequently added.

Waterlooville became part of the Borough of Havant and Waterloo in 1932. The borough also included Hayling Island to the south, and Warblington and Emsworth to the east. The area had been served by an enlarged Union Workhouse since 1834 and counted many ex-servicemen among its inmates. Women and children were housed separately in those pious times and given dreary jobs like grinding up hemp on a spike in return for basic board and lodging. Well-to-do ratepayers often resented the burden of paying for the transient poor. Hardship during the protectionist 1830s was considerable, and relatively speaking the

1930s were not much better, though there had been some progress toward basic education, unemployment insurance and health care. Ex-servicemen tramping through the district in search of work was again a familiar sight.

The build-up to another war in 1939 perked things up a bit. I grew up in a poor family not many years after that war ended. It was an age of high expectation, when politicians promised even more 'Homes fit for Heroes' than Lloyd George had done after the First World War. Promises were bandied about by competing parties, all in the hope of votes and power, at a time when the country was nearly bankrupt. Portsmouth City Council bought Sir Freddie Fitzwygram's Leigh Park Estate in 1946, demolished his house and went on to build council houses for a post-war generation who, it might be said, had earned the right to a little peace and comfort after so much sacrifice.

But it turned out to be a post-war age of confusion. Massive possibilities opened up, but financial decisions were difficult to make. How much would the rich pay in taxes before their spirit of enterprise was destroyed? What might ordinary people really expect? Equality of opportunity is, after all, a contradiction in terms. Havant and Portsmouth's homeless and badly housed got Leigh Park. The first generation into the park brought many social problems with them and it took a generation at least to settle down and find an identity. In the 1990s Havant got the Meridian Centre and lost a number of small specialist and eccentric shops. Some people say the Centre came too late in an age biased towards out of town shopping centres.

Vestiges of the past survive in such places as Hayling's moated Manor House. In Havant there is the ruined terrace overlooking the great lake of Leigh Park – remnant of an age when opening the great grounds for a fête or granting land in New Lane for allotments was enough to please the poor. Nowadays people want so much more and the old religious certainties have gone.

Still I smile when I look back on my first tours of Havant's sites of the past and sights of what was then its present. I was with Roger, a tax office colleague of about my age and with his own sense of the dramatic. We were one of the two-man teams (how horribly sexist it all was then!) sent to collect the wages for the clerical assistants from the National Westminster Bank on the corner of North Street. Roger insisted on taking a roundabout route in case we were being followed by bandits. We must have looked in every shop window and walked almost to Emsworth before shooting back to collect the money and make a dash for it back to the tax office. What terrible criminal times we lived in, and now some say it's worse. But I wonder if it's really any worse than all those golden olden days. It's difficult to know. A sensible person can only wonder.

Robert Cook, June 1996

Looking across the lake at Leigh Park, from the site of the old grand house. The lake had been a picture, with ornamental gardens and islands connected by little bridges and inspired by owner Sir George Staunton's travels with the East India Company. (V. Church)

GOING BACK

*Another 'Empire' long gone – the cinema at Havant
which opened in 1913. (Thor Halley)*

Havant station after the 1938 rebuild shows hints of Charles Holden's 'house style', made famous on the London Underground in the 1930s. My first exit from this station was in July 1974, having travelled nearly 150 miles to be reunited with my young lover. Fresh out of university and hell-bent on not finding a suitable career, I was a self-conscious romantic with a sense of doom. My obsession with Samuel Beckett's poetry and Neil Young's songs soon wore on my girlfriend's nerves and I was inevitably left to find new friends. Fortunately there were other young people in the area as daft as me! Those were the last of the real 'hippy days'. I used to ride miles to and from Havant station, carrying my guitar and writing doggerel on the insides of my empty cigarette packets. Here is an awful remnant from the summer of 1975.

> A young lover broods on Havant-bound train.
> Counting the miles before he'll see her again,
> Calling at Guildford and Godalming too,
> all through the South Downs the boy misses the view.
> He just cannot wait to see her again,
> that's why he's riding the Havant-bound train.
> At last there's the factories north of town,
> soon he'll see her wearing a long 'hippy gown'.
> There she is waiting by the station door,
> for another young lover who'd become such a bore!

Tax office staff at Elmleigh Road in the early 1970s. By the time I joined the team in 1975 they had moved into Park Road South. I think I can spot my old friend Barbara Privett (painter to my poet) fourth from the left in the centre row, behind the man with glasses. All the rest seem to have left before my arrival – perhaps they'd heard I was coming! This building continued to house social security staff after the Inland Revenue moved out. As I had to wait one month for a salary cheque, I called at Elmleigh Road benefit office for help toward my rent. It was my lucky day. The lady on reception was Jean Neal, who not only organized my giro but arranged for me to rent her back bedroom in Lymbourne Road – it must have been my good looks! Anyway this road was very handy for the Empire cinema which was almost opposite in East Street. Small and quaint, it was just the place to get lost in a dream world. The best picture I saw there was 'One flew over the cuckoo's nest'. The story implied that the inmates of a lunatic asylum were saner than their guards and therapists. It was raining when I came out and I told my girlfriend to wait under the cinema portico so she did not get her nice evening dress wet. Off I went, like an old-fashioned gent, to fetch my old Mini. Proudly I pulled up in East Street, held open the car door and beckoned her toward me. But I had forgotten the cracked wheel arch on the front passenger side. Every puddle we hit on the way back to her house might as well have been a bucket of water thrown up at her. (M. Hudson)

Havant tax officials gather outside the Park Road office building, now the site of the bus station. Is it the 'invisible man' or the ghost of Fred Eavis who seems to be standing between them? The occasion was the Queen's Silver Jubilee in 1977. Jill Eyre, far left, sports the flared fashions of the day and Havant stalwart Muriel Hudson, is sixth from left. Rumour has it that Muriel enjoyed working for the Inland Revenue almost as much as I did! (M. Hudson)

Myself and son Kieran on a nostalgic visit to my old haunts in 1988. I noticed that the doorway lettering on the old tax office had been tampered with and thought sadly how little respect people seem to have nowadays for great traditions like paying taxes! I remember the glory days with Fred Eavis striking fear into his underlings, striding officer-like through this doorway, cap and sports jacket in all weathers and long mac in winter. He was a great fellow who once told me I could never leave because graduates like me weren't fit for much else and probably not even fit for the revenue. He was a great joker! (N. Cook)

Here I am again, casting a sentimental eye toward my old Lymbourne Road lodgings in 1988. I think I preferred it as it was in my day, with no tar, just a rough track. But I am told that it is now a haven for the upwardly mobile and has to accommodate many more cars. My worst memory of living here is of landlady Jean waking me up on Sunday morning by playing her 'Singalonga Max' records very loudly on her radiogram. By that time her husband Bill would be at the bottom of his garden admiring his prize pigeons – a fine Havant tradition, the Havant Fanciers show being held in the nearby Town Hall. (N. Cook)

Nicola Cook poses outside St Faith's church hall where she attended her first playgroup session in the early 1960s: 'I can remember sitting at an easel painting a Christmas tree picture, with lots of baubles. This lady came up behind me saying "What a lovely picture". Then for some reason I painted it all over in black so they couldn't see it. They thought I'd ruined it, but I knew it was still there, safely hidden,' she said. (R. Cook)

I rather liked my beer in Havant days and tried most of the local pubs. I remember my landlady's alarm when I said I was going to visit The Bear. 'That's where they talk money and they mean it,' she said. The Bear has over 200 years of history: at one time known as The Black Bear, it sometimes served as courthouse for the Petty Sessions. The Duke of Norfolk dined there in 1824 after opening Hayling's first road bridge. Queen Victoria, en route to Portsmouth, is said to have changed horses there in 1840. (V. Church)

The Old House at Home, South Street, photographed in the early 1960s. But for the car and bicycles this might be a scene from the sixteenth century from which this building dates – it was the only half-timbered building to survive the 'great fire' of 1760. The MG Magnette, left of picture, reminds me of tax office colleague John Negus who owned a red one. Living in Leigh Park, he told me, forced him to take the extreme security measure of wiring it to the mains overnight. I don't know whether he was joking but I was quite shocked! (M. Hudson)

Apologies for the quality of this picture but I was riding along Elmleigh Road in the back seat of a car, nursing a broken leg, when I took it and could not get a good angle. This Sunday afternoon tricyclist reminded me of the Portsmouth Polytechnic lecturer I met in the Old House at Home in the winter of 1975. Through open pub curtains I watched the dark and caped figure parking his large trike on the pavement and stared brazenly as a piercing-eyed man with Heathcliffe-style hair entered the bar. With a sweep of a hand he pulled a gleaming tankard from under his cape and it was duly filled. I quickly engaged this unusual person in conversation and learned many things, including that he was fascinated by Alice in Wonderland. But I don't suppose this is the same man in the picture! (R. Cook)

Sandleford Road, Leigh Park, 1975. My friend Vernon Church came to live here when he transferred from the Inland Revenue in London. There was a huge movement of staff into the area in those days as large-scale computerization was planned. The first big centre was South 1 at Hilsea. But with a change of government the programme lost momentum and Vernon ended up in Havant with me. It was a tax man's backwater, but we had some good times. (V. Church)

Here is one of those good times – one of our extended Wednesday lunchbreaks at Vernon's Sandleford Road home in 1976. We had cheese on toast and a little too much to drink! Eventually I also moved on to the estate, just up the road in Inkpen Walk, close to the scene of a famous Leigh Park murder (*see* p. 109). (V. Church)

Inkpen Walk was good for the open countryside beyond. Once I decided to reform, I used to run for miles in the woods and found some peace there. Staunton Country Park is in the neighbourhood, providing a thousand acres of parkland. The land used to belong to horticulturalist and orientalist Sir George Staunton. The well-restored glasshouses include the lilyhouse, containing giant *Victoria amazonica*. There are also tropical flowers, fruit, magnificent lilies and tree-frogs. (R. Cook)

Dave Evans's painting of the 'Hayling Billy' train crossing the Mulberry pontoons over Langston Water has been printed on Christmas cards for the Portsmouth Hospitals Rocky Appeal. The appeal is being coordinated by Mick Lyons to raise £2 million pounds for a magnetic resonance imaging scanner. It's a shame there wasn't an appeal for money to save this old bridge which was no more than a few rotting stumps when I arrived in Havant. I could see part of the railway cutting leading to Langstone from my Lymbourne Road back bedroom and was moved to compose the following:

They called it the 'Billy', the train that went past,
trying so hard, but never quite fast.
Out of the station and hard round the bend,
and the kids on board would sometimes pretend
the train they were riding went to the Wild West,
where they could shoot baddies, or at least do their
        best.

Over the bridge, the spindly mile,
watching the seagulls and crossing the piles.
Looking at boats that had silly names,
little minds planning a day's fun and games.
Onto the island where Indians might roam,
out in the wilds a long way from home.

This was the land way over the sea,
with cleanest of beaches, a land of the free.
They'd leave the train hissing and letting off steam
and spend all day in a happy dream.

Now it's all over, the train is no more,
life is so different, the kids say 'a bore'.
The bridge had to go to save so much money,
and the traffic jams grew, it really is funny.

I live in a room with nothing to do,
but sit, look and listen, enjoying the view.
Look as I might, there's nothing to see
to fill in the space where the rails used to be.
Only the grass and a little old fence,
where smoke used to puff, sometimes quite dense.

I live in a room where there's nothing to hear,
this time or next time, whatever the year.
Now the railway has gone, the passengers too,
I live in a room with nothing to view.
Lymbourne's back yards have lost the sweet sound
of clattering old Billy's wheels going round.

Newcomer Vernon Church on the beach at Hayling with his wife Sylvia in 1975. Like many, he found Havant an ideal location for his family. (C. Church)

A self-service fuel station designed for today's fast efficiency-loving people. It's a far cry from Tommy Marshall's creaky old Havant Garage which stood on this Park Road site until the late 1970s. I remember Tommy offering to buy me a drink in the Homewell pub. It was my first night living in town and he was buying a round. I said, 'You can't buy me a drink, I'm a stranger.' Little Tommy scrutinized me through his specs and said, 'A pint for the stranger.' (V. Church)

This is September 1970 and Clinton Dennison (right) and Harold Pycroft are taking it slow, admiring the old cobblestone wall alongside Harold's property in Woodgaston Lane, Hayling Island. Harold, a master brickmaker, knew a good wall when he saw one. This one was 300 ft long and comprised some 45,000 cobbles, most of which were carried up from the harbour in fishermen's baskets; it was built in about 1860 by George Ogburn for William Rogers. (Noel Pycroft).

This was William Stone's house which replaced Sir George Staunton's original Leigh Park mansion. It survived until 1959 when Portsmouth Corporation decided to turn their Leigh Park estate into the second largest council housing estate in Britain. The plan was mainly to rehouse the Portsmouth overspill and the social and economic impact on the tiny market town of Havant, barely a mile to the south, was considerable. Insufficient thought was given toward ways of creating a sense of community among the mainly young people being rehoused and in the early days the estate became notorious for social problems. When I lived there I was oblivious to the problems, though I might have been one of the nuisances, playing my electric guitar so loud that the charming divorcée next door complained. She eventually emigrated to the USA, but I don't think that had anything to do with me! The walls between the units were so thin, it was possible to hear all sorts of things. But there were a lot of people to be rehoused and costs had to be cut (see p. 123). (V. Church)

CALLED TO ARMS

*'Dobie Timp', alias Havant's Dick Little of the
Hampshire Regiment awaiting troop transport to Egypt
in 1940.*

When Havant and Waterloo Urban District Council was formed, a second fire engine was purchased to be based at Waterlooville. The Havant machine was based at Park Road North. When war broke out in 1939, a National Fire Service was created and many men were called on to join the Auxiliary Fire Service. The group shown here was photographed in Havant in 1939. Dick Little (centre), joined the fire service before the outbreak of war. He said, 'War was imminent and Portsmouth was expected to take a beating. Our first base was a dilapidated garage in a large garden in east Havant. It hadn't been used for years and took days to make habitable. My girl used to come around in the evenings. We played cards – American rummy was in fashion and we were called "the Rummy Boys". This carried on until I was called up into the 1st Battalion Hampshire Regiment. While I was with the fire brigade we attended two small incidents and got ticked off by the Fire Chief. We swear it was because he didn't like us making any monetary gain and his losing out – we got paid a fixed fee for each call-out, as well as our retainer, but of course the regular fire service wanted all the action.' The cups in this picture were won at a local fete in 1939. (R. Little)

The fire service was expanded because heavy bombing and civilian casualties were expected on a large scale in strategic areas, such as Portsmouth Dockyard, only a few miles to the south. This is the first aid post at St Faith's, Havant, reinforced with anti-blast sandbags. It was expected to serve up to 500 people, and was staffed by a nurse, doctor and auxiliaries. (*Portsmouth News*)

The Home Guard on the look-out outside Stents leather glove factory, Bedhampton, Havant. In peacetime Jesse Hunt remembers living nearby: 'The factory had an awful smell about it.' But there were more overwhelming sensations about when this wartime picture was taken in August 1940 – the Battle of Britain had already started. The Home Guard was originally the Local Defence Volunteers (LDV). This was soon corrupted to 'Look, Duck and Vanish' – given the paucity of their training and weapons that might have been a wise strategy if they had ever been tested in battle. (*Portsmouth News*)

Mrs Armitage and her daughter Minnie Gertrude, shown here in 1890, needed no lessons on 'power dressing'. They could have taught the cast of 'Dynasty' a few lessons on style. The young lady enjoyed a long life and was unperturbed by the events of the Second World War. Tony Hill recalls her as his 'Nanny Newland' and remembers the day in August 1940 when 'Nanny had been to the matinee at the Empire Cinema and was on her way home to Denvilles at about 4.30 p.m. At this moment a German plane came in over Bell Air, dropping bombs. It killed Mr Small the builder and must have been following the London–Brighton railway line. Nanny had got to the station and was waiting at the level-crossing gates. She sheltered under her umbrella as it went over, shooting at the signal box. A whole wall was knocked down at Fairfield School. At our home in Denvilles the Venetian blind and windows were blown in. I remember terrific warmth and glass flying everywhere. I was about eight. We kids competed to see who could find the biggest piece of shrapnel. We took the war in our stride because we grew up with it. There was an ack-ack [anti-aircraft] gun on the roundabout and a searchlight near the incinerator site. Grandfather built a dug-out in the garden covered with sleepers. Sirens used to wail a lot. I remember seeing the silhouette of a flying bomb through the curtains one night. All you wanted to hear was that its motor was running. When it stopped it fell out of the sky.' (A. Hill)

The attack on Nanny Newland and builder Small was quickly avenged, as this picture testifies. The Junkers was shot down and crashed near Woodberry Lane, Rowlands Castle. (*Portsmouth News*)

The British, great ones for fair play, despatched these two angels of mercy to the crash, but the three crewmen were already dead, and no doubt being ministered to by other angels. (*Portsmouth News*)

One Second World War naval veteran told me: 'Going away to the Navy was an exciting change from town life. I was a grocer's delivery boy when I volunteered at 17. But when it started getting rough I started wishing for my mother.' These young boys of 1941 don't all seem sure about their Christmas cheer on Hayling Island. Their expressions have more hints of 1960s holiday camp dwellers! (*Portsmouth News*)

Young men had to grow up fast during the Second World War. As of old, when the nation was threatened, they were expected to become warriors. Here is Dick Little just before the Siege of Malta in 1941. He said: 'Malta is about the size of the Isle of Wight. Germans dropped bombs in sticks of four chained together. They put four craters close to me. The suction of the blast pulled all the air out of my body. I thought, my God I'm going to explode. The noise and screaming was terrible. It was night time at the top of the village on the ack-ack site. Someone said, "you're wanted, there's seven or eight in a hole under a direct hit". We had to get the bits of body out. You never forgot it. But we had to carry on.' (*Portsmouth News*)

This ack-ack battery was closer to home on Hayling Island. It was destroyed by a direct hit with heavy loss of life during a raid in April 1941. (*Portsmouth News*)

Whether through stray bombs or German intent, Hayling Island was too close to Portsmouth to avoid taking a pounding. This was West Town in April 1941, following the same raid mentioned above. (*Portsmouth News*)

After Dick Little's close call at Malta, he was allowed to send a telegram home to Havant. He sent six words to his sweetheart Gwen Newland: 'Will you marry me? Love Dick.' He got his answer on the boat and they were married in Havant on 19 November 1943. (R. Little)

Wedding celebrations were not long over before Dick was back in training for D-Day landings, from a base at Studland Bay. 'We came out to simulate landings on Hayling Island. I was doing this when I saw Americans tossing boxes of corned beef off boats. They said they'd got too much. I persuaded them to let me have some and filled the panniers on my motorbike. I took it home to Gwen. Corned beef was like gold then, with rationing on,' said Dick. Hence there were many things to celebrate when this picture was taken at Denvilles on VE-Day 1945 – sadly an end to rationing was not one of them. (A. Hill)

OLD WAYS

Havant 'Going West' — West Street, c. 1910.

This gatehouse tower, pictured in about 1908, is a remnant of Warblington Castle. King Henry VIII's cousin Margaret Pole, Countess of Salisbury, who owned the castle, had her head hacked off while standing at the gallows in 1541 because she refused to accept the King's marriage to Ann Boleyn and his self-appointment as head of a new English Church. William, Earl of Southampton, became steward of her manors. After his death Warblington passed to Richard Cotton, Comptroller of the King's household. The castle was destroyed by Cromwell's men during the English Civil War. We think we live in violent times! (V. Church)

South Street, c. 1900. St Faith's Church is just visible on the left. South Street became much busier in the age of the motor car, but the much-needed bypass built in 1965 restored something of its olde worlde tranquillity. It used to link up with Langstone's prehistoric Wadeway to Hayling. (R. Little)

An engraving showing a wind pump at the Salterns in the Hundred of Bosmere, Hayling. A saltern is a salt-works using pools for the natural evaporation of sea water. Salt traders would carry salt inland; it was particularly important for preserving beef in brine tubs in the days before refrigerators. (M. Hudson)

Belmont House, Bedhampton, in the years before the Royal Navy's tented camps graced the lawns and parkland during the Second World War. It doesn't look very attractive from the outside but was sumptuous within, symbolic of the power and prestige enjoyed by a mighty few. (V. Church)

A jolly and playful scene at Stansted Avenue, Rowlands Castle, on the northern edge of the parish, photographed in about 1900. The avenue, extending for over two miles, was a perfect recreation space for children, in an age when children could stray with little fear of molestation. But they faced other hazards, then. (J. Ounsworth)

A pony and trap clip-clopping past the blacksmith's shop in Havant, en route to Emsworth, *c.* 1907. Nowadays cars speed their way past via a concrete flyover. (R. Cook)

Jesus was the Holy Shepherd and the church was once home to his flock. Thus the Church became the cement holding society together. King Henry VIII was the first to dilute the mixture and it has been crumbling ever since. This building, St Peter's at Northney, dates back to the good old days of the twelfth century and its structure has changed little since then. Reputedly, its three bells give the oldest peal in England. William Burrows and Noel Pycroft erected the weather vane. (M. Hudson)

St Mary's Parish Church on South Hayling is slightly younger and noticeably larger than St Peter's. It also shows a variety of styles following various additions and alterations. The three bells were sold to cover repairs in 1805. A third, more southerly, church was apparently lost through coastal erosion. Stonework has been recovered in an area called Church Rocks. (M. Hudson)

You can no longer drive sheep down the road like this lot at Bedhampton Crossing gates in about 1907. Like the human flock, there are too many distractions and it would be difficult to keep them on the chosen path. There's also no market in Havant to drive them to. (V. Church)

The proper thing to do after church on the Sabbath was to take a walk in your Sunday best, as this young lady seems to be doing. She is passing the pond at Warblington. (V. Church)

North Street, shown here in about 1910, has been rather altered by developments in the late 1980s but is still recognizable from this picture. Photographer and inventor William Scorer ran a studio and shop along here until his death in 1929. He patented cameras, including ones for aerial photography and X-rays. In 1900 he opened the National Telephone Company. Telephones seem to have been in the family blood – both his daughters worked as exchange supervisors. Mr Scorer also mended barometers and cinema equipment.

The two ladies passing the post office in West Street in about 1919 look rather Edwardian and unliberated. But they have the vote now and change will be rapid. This post office housed a telephone exchange for trunk calls. (V. Church)

West Street, *c.* 1910. It was as busy with shoppers then as it is today. Penny farthing riders have always been a marvel to me. How do they get on and off, and why were bicycles ever designed in such a silly way? Even sillier, this road had to cope with heavy through-traffic right up to the 1960s.

Two men of fine style and bearing pass the Old House at Home in South Street in 1912. Meanwhile a new-fangled motor car occupies the cross-roads. On the right is an advert for a more environmentally friendly means of transport – bicycles. The great Wadham Stringer (later Wadham Kenning) motor vehicle business began in Havant with one of the Wadham brothers working in Jones's cycle shop in 1894. (V. Church)

Pumping water up from wells was still the norm for obtaining water when this picture was taken, *c.* 1914. Havant is well known for its springs to the south-east of West Street. This area suffered regular flooding until the Portsmouth Water Company sank enough boreholes and laid water mains to draw the water away. (V. Church)

Before the Portsmouth Water Company laid on a mains supply from Havant in 1925, Hayling Island relied on this water tower and pumping station. The station started working on Hayling in 1895 and eventually outlived its usefulness, being demolished in 1952. (V. Church)

The fresh spring water from the South Downs was good for two small industries: growing watercress in Lymbourne Stream and parchment-making, as shown here in 1926. The fresh water drained off the South Downs, supplying the springs and good grazing. The sheep were slaughtered and skinned, and their skins soaked in lime water, as shown here, then scraped free of fat and stretched. A local industry since Roman times, the parchment makers of Havant are said to have supplied their famous pure white parchment for both the Magna Carta and Versailles Treaty. The rise of synthetic materials in the 1930s destroyed the industry. (V. Church)

Brickmaking on North Hayling in the late 1930s. This is the traditional hand way of making them, as opposed to the cheap Fletton mass-production method used by the London Brick Company (*see* p. 89). Flettons used Lower Oxford Clay from depths of 90 ft which contained enough carbon virtually to fire itself as long as the kilns didn't go out. Fletton clay is so hard that it needs powerful presses to shape it. These men are using yellow brick earth, from nearer the surface. It is mixed into a paste called pug and then moulded (*see* pp. 111, 112, 113). (N. Pycroft)

The Little family collected tolls at the new toll bridge house at Langstone in 1824. Their barge business, carrying shingle, coal and timber, was founded in 1842. This picture shows the barges at Langstone in about 1890. Dick Little recalls: 'When the barges came in they got close up to the quayside wall. Men in the hold threw the shingle on to the deck and then it was thrown on to the quay.' Built by the Hayling Bridge and Causeway Company who had built a railway link to Havant, the quays were leased to the Littles for £300 per year. Business was looking up and was further boosted by the First World War. (R. Little)

The aircraft industry, exemplified here by this Bristol Box Kite on Southern Hayling in 1911, was also looking up as war tensions increased. The Crescent in the background was symbolic of the island's aspirations to be a high-class resort. But war changed all that. By the 1930s Nevil Shute Norway was living in the area and, encouraged by Portsmouth Council's forward-looking business incentives, chose to move his Airspeed aeroplane company to Portsmouth Airport. At that time there was also a plan to make Langstone a base for flying boats going to and from the Commonwealth. (V. Church)

Jimmy Usher was an odd-job man of repute and lived in Woodgaston Lane, Hayling Island. His home was an old Portsmouth Corporation Tramcar. This picture was taken in the orchard of Woodgaston Cottage in 1925. When he died in Havant workhouse in 1934, the villagers raised a collection to buy him a headstone. (N. Pycroft)

Hayling is now a trendy place to live and the fields are diminishing. This view is Elm Grove in the 1920s. The houses became shops and the field on the left was taken to make way for a public library, a fire station and the pub called the 'Hayling Billy'. The front of the pub was graced with *Newington*, a retired 'Hayling Billy' locomotive. *Newington* has been restored and is now working on the Isle of Wight. (N. Cook)

Beachland Lodge, South Hayling, in the early 1900s. Like the Crescent (*see* p. 37), it was part of a plan to give Hayling an upmarket image and attract Cheltenham Spa types. The building hints at Ancient Greek culture and housed a library, art gallery and games room. But, as my old Havant landlady used to say, 'breeding will out' – and the building was replaced by an ice-cream kiosk! (R. Little)

Langstone Mill during the 'Great Freeze' of 1895. The waters around the mill have frozen many times, but most famously in 1963. In February 1979 *The News* reported that 'a touch of the tundra came to Langstone at the weekend when the receding tide froze in its tracks'. During the 1930s Nevil Shute was a regular visitor here during his association with owner and artist Flora Twort. But their relationship never warmed toward romance. (M. Hudson)

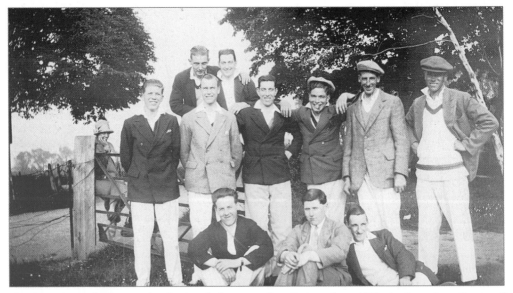

Havant cricketers looking cool and relaxed after a match at Emsworth, *c.* 1920. As the writer of some of the world's worst poems, I once observed: 'Cricket lovely cricket, how I would miss it, bat, ball and run, tea and currant bun, Englishman's disease, as gentle as the breeze.' (J. Hunt)

The Look-out at Langstone was built as part of the battle against vicious smugglers which started in the eighteenth century. Pook Lane, in this area, may have originally been called Spook Lane because of its association with smugglers. This picture was taken in about 1919, but it was free trade rather than this station or the Royal Navy Patrols which killed smuggling in the 1840s. Before that Langstone Mill was used as a store for contraband and its sails were used for signalling. Wool was smuggled out; whisky, tea, lace and silk were smuggled in. (M. Hudson)

Langstone Bridge Toll House, *c.* 1890. The Little family fortunes began here with Albert Little in 1824. Dick Little's father took redundancy from Portsmouth Dockyard and joined his brother Graham in the family firm. Dick says, 'He was asked to take responsibility for two German submarines from World War One, coming into Pook Lane Quay to be cut up into small pieces to make a barrier against the tide which was eroding the foreshore. It lasted years.' (M. Hudson)

The Little family barges stand proudly on the quay, *c.* 1900. Dick remembers growing up in the 1930s when his father and uncle Graham had a small office on the quay: 'It was full of little mysteries and intricacies, drawers and things. Between ages 11 and 13, I used to go regularly on the boats all summer. These days shingle barges are loaded from dredgers at Portsmouth. In the old days we would pull in and pick up shingle and sand while the tide was out.' (R. Little)

Langstone Regatta in 1908 was a popular and lively event. Sadly, by July 1976 the *Hampshire Telegraph* had to report Portsmouth ecologist F. Haynes's question: 'Birds or people? is that the only choice we face – over the future of Langstone Harbour'. Around 9 million gallons of effluent were then poured into the harbour, 'greatly to the liking of green seaweed (*Entesmorpha*) growing there because it is spreading steadily.' John Hudson of *The Lookout* commented at the time: 'The upper reaches of the harbour are being choked . . . instead of looking out onto grey mud the area is covered green as a lawn.' (M. Hudson)

Langstone Harbour in the late 1940s, still looking as Heaven might. Douglas Hickson captured the atmosphere in the *Hampshire Telegraph* in February 1975: 'Langstone village in the early morning when the tide begins to flood and a sunshine-filtered mist hangs lazily around dew-wet boats rocking gently at moorings and gliding swans cause no ripple . . . Langstone then is a place of pure peace and tranquillity.' (M. Hudson)

But Langstone in this 1912 Regatta picture is all go, as the four oar racers get ready to make waves. (M. Hudson)

This scene shows some of the gathering enjoying the more leisurely side of the sport at Langstone Regatta in 1912. At this time Langstone was very much a working harbour. Over the years there has been some conflict between the fishing and leisure activities in the neighbouring harbours of Chichester and Langstone. Vincent Tune, an Emsworth fisherman, responded to Surrey sailor Graham Innes's letter to *The News* (November 1977) thus: 'If we have such thoughtless people as Mr Innes within the harbour who obviously think that fishermen interfere with yachting, I suggest he takes his yacht back to sail on the quiet lakes of Surrey.' (M. Hudson)

Graham Little of the famous Langstone family operated this boat when the picture was taken in 1912. Dick Little recalls: 'At one time she made regular trips with gravel from Langstone to ports along the coast, returning with coal or whatever. After that she made regular trips to the Isle of Wight taking sand and gravel and returning with other cargoes. The boat's heydays were holiday times, making trips with as many locals as could get on board.' The barge was abandoned in 1926 and became a hulk in Langstone Harbour. (R. Little)

The storm clouds of war were gathering over Europe when this picture was taken outside Havant station in 1913. Manoeuvres were taking place throughout Britain and this cycling detachment of the 9th Hampshire Regiment looked like a real menace to the enemy! (V. Church)

This is the 9.20 a.m. mixed goods train passing the old wharf siding with goods wagons loose coupled on the back, 29 July 1931. The Hayling Road bridge had a 6 ton 6 cwt weight limit and so the railway was vital for getting heavy goods on and off the island. Dick Little remembers Station Master Jordan: 'He was a Scot. As a boy in the 1930s I was throwing stones and broke a Langstone station lamp. Over the next three weeks I got so uptight I went round behind the signal box on the way home from school and said to Mr Jordan, "I broke your lamp." He said, 'I know you did. I was waiting for you to come and apologize. Now you have I won't grumble."' (M. Hudson)

The only way to deal with Havant's natural tendency to flood was lay good drains, as shown here in North Street early this century. Building workers worked even harder in this pre-JCB age and many road and drain improvements were undertaken to relieve unemployment during the 1930s.

A finely dressed gathering at one of Havant's last sports days in the park before the First World War. Running races for 'pots' and prizes was popular in Edwardian times, but in spite of the enthusiasm for sport, it was difficult to find enough fit young men for the carnage that began in 1914.

The post office moved, along with the telephone exchange, into East Street in 1936. It is one of two buildings carrying Edward VIII's emblem and is a symbol of a new Edwardian age that didn't quite happen. The uncrowned King was judged immoral for pursuing his love for a divorced woman, Wallis Simpson. He abdicated and was later accused of collaborating with the enemy during the war. Maybe his example nudged us toward the moral uncertainties of the present. The post office has since moved into a more cost-effective unit at the Meridian Centre. (R. Cook)

Looking like a time before the 1938 electrification (electric trials began in 1937), this T9 locomotive, number 30718, arrives at Havant on 3 May 1953 with a special train. Muriel Hudson (née Burrows) recalls her 1930s schoolgirl days travelling by steam train to Petersfield Girls' high school: 'The school was very strict about keeping us away from boys. Ron Read was boys' prefect on the train. He was supposed to keep the sexes apart but he always jumped into a compartment with us girls. And we used to feed boys in through our carriage windows while we were in the tunnel.' The railway was first built on speculation by Thomas Brassey, a man who believed in keeping his navvies in order with some religious education. His railway building Act went through Parliament in 1853 and his company was called the Direct Portsmouth Railway (from London). To travel south beyond Havant he needed running powers over London, Brighton & South Coast tracks to Hilsea. The new railway was ready for twelve months before the House of Lords agreed to this. The first train was due on 1 January 1859 but the Brighton company sent navvies to remove the joining rails and they chained an old Bury engine to the diamond crossing. Brassey sent his own navvies into the famous 'Battle of Havant' to resolve the matter, but they got the worst of the fisticuffs. The dispute went to arbitration and was resolved in Brassey's favour. There then followed a fare war. (B.K.B. Green)

HAPPY DAYS

Girls and boys come out to play beside the beach huts,
beside the sea at Hayling, c. 1952. (R. Little)

Before the 'never had it so good' post-war years, people say they still had fun, the truth of which perhaps shows in this Havant scene from 1907. The parade is passing the Union Workhouse in West Street, raising money for local hospitals. But the decision to build Havant Memorial Hospital was not made until the First World War had officially ended in 1919 and the first sod was not cut until 16 November 1927. Health care had a long way to go and the poor had a great struggle to get any at all.

Jess Hunt and his sister Dolly, *c.* 1912. Jess said: 'My father came here to work the signal box for the London, Brighton & South Coast railway. He left my mother for another woman. I was 14 years old and there were eight children in our family. I became the breadwinner. We lived in Bedhampton Lane down by the railway gates. That was the poor quarter. Boys used to go to school barefoot. There were plenty of kids down there but not one of them got into trouble. Course there was no television then. People just went to bed. That's why there were so many kids!' (J. Hunt)

Schoolboy Dick Little in the 1930s. He said:
'I used to enjoy going out on the barges, looking
for the best spots for shingle in Hayling Bay. My
cousin, a Londoner, used to come down in
summer. Looking back on those times, he'd say,
"Do you remember the old drinks of cocoa we
had?" It was a solid sort of chocolate and never
good until you could stand the spoon up in it. We
brewed it on the boat. It was black by the time it
was ready. All that was left behind on leaving
school. I went to Coates in Waterlooville Road,
earning 7s 6d a week as a paper boy. Then Edgar
Oughton offered me an assistant's job at
International Stores for 15s a week. I would be
there until 2 a.m. in the morning. Dad didn't like
that and I moved to the Co-op until just before
the war.' (R. Little)

Gwen Newland (left) and a schoolfriend in the
1930s, when girls were taught to be girls. Jesse
Hunt remembers: 'There were two schools in
Brockhampton Lane. One was for boys and one
for girls. There was also a little Catholic girls'
school in West Street. In those days I wouldn't
use the toilets – they stank. We played rougher
games than the girls, like one team of boys
standing up against a wall and the other team
would jump on top of them and try to make
them collapse.' (G. Little)

Havant Wednesday Football Club, 1928/29. Wednesday was early closing day in Havant, giving the men time off to play football – hence the club name.

Havant Wednesday Football Club, 1930s. Jesse Hunt, a local barber, is second from the right in the front row. He grew up playing football like most boys but remembers it being a cleaner game. 'Children were so different then. Boys were boys and girls were girls. We had discipline. One of our teachers was called Freddie Farthing. He played for Havant Rovers and was a smashing bloke.' (J. Hunt)

The Church took a keen interest in boys' welfare – here is the vicar with St Faith's Football Club, photographed during the 1928/29 season. (J. Hunt)

Gracie Joan Ponting, daughter of the famous London store proprietor, looks a good sport against this local woodland background in about 1923. She is taking time off from her nursing duties at the St Andrews Home which was next to the lifeboat station on Hayling Island. She said: 'We helped launch the lifeboat and pull it back into the station. I was seventeen, dealing with TB and paralysis patients from babies up to 21-year-olds. They slept in shelters which had only sailcloth at both ends, and were very cold in winter. The matron, Miss Katherine Twining, was strict but fair. We had little social life. There was only one pub and a little general store. Some girls didn't get much financial support from their families, and £1 a month salary didn't go far.' (W. Barton)

Bowling was popular at Bell Air early this century, but the sport's image has become more youthful over the years since television discovered it. This is a more traditional gathering of the Havant British Legion Club bowls team in 1958. (J. Hunt)

The young lady members of Bedhampton badminton club were in safe hands here with the vicar, c. 1937. I wonder if Jesse Hunt (back row, second from right) is responsible for all the men having such sensible hair cuts! Jesse started out delivering for a cycle shop at 14 years old and ended up working long hours as an apprentice hairdresser. But he still found time for a lot of exercise! (J. Hunt)

Havant Rovers Veterans in 1952, posed by the old recreation ground pavilion which was financed by subscriptions from Havant tradesmen. The pavilion's opening in 1890 was celebrated with bands playing and a cricket match between Havant Local Board Veterans and Portsmouth Town Councillors. The home team won. (J. Hunt)

Gwen Little, looking stylish in spite of clothes rationing, at Langstone in 1944. Gwen met husband Dick in the Empire cinema. Dick said: 'We met in the dark. The cashier said, "If you go to the cinema tonight and I sit you next to a friend of mine, is it worth it?" I said, "I don't know." Anyway it was. Every holiday time there was a fair in Star Meadow and we went. It was gone ten before we got home, wandering slowly. Her father was waiting and said, "Come on, don't hang about."' Gwen worked in the office at Stents during the war, when the firm was busy making flying suits and gloves. (G. Little)

Youngsters growing up around Havant didn't need a municipal pool to learn to swim. Dick Little is taking a dip here in Lymbourne, in the late 1930s, when hard work was normal and pleasure was easy and simple. Dick said: 'We cycled into the country. I was in Portsmouth Cyclist Touring Club. I cycled all the way to Weston-super-Mare.' (R. Little)

But there were few things Dick enjoyed more than getting out in the family barges, looking for shingle. This is Sandy Point on Hayling Island, looking a bit the worse for wear after the Second World War. Dick recalls: 'As a boy my brother and I would take our boat *Langstone* out. She had an engine. We'd go toward Hayling Bay by the old hospital at Sandy Point. All you saw was an area of sea. We'd take marks from various points. The barge was anchored. When the tide went out and the shingle showed, we put the plank down to wheel the big barrow down to the shingle. I fell off the plank many times. It took a while, up and down the plank, to load the hold with 30 tons. We worked like mad before the tide returned.' (M. Hudson)

'Peace in our time.' Gwen Little and her
mother-in-law in the garden at Langstone, 1945.
(R. Little)

Havant policeman and tennis champion Tony Hill
posing for the camera in the garden at Denvilles. Tony
was a member of the élite Denvilles Tennis Club and
his dedication to the sport led him to the finals of the
national police tennis tournament several times.
Competing at Bedford in June 1972, he won the
singles title for the South East Region Police Athletics
Association and went on to the finals in Manchester.
(R. Little)

Tony demonstrates his service. The competition in this case was photographic, as David Dew entered this shot – entitled 'The Service' – in a Horndean Camera Club competition in October 1982. He ought to have called it 'The long arm of the law!' (A. Hill/D. Dew)

Dick Little mowing the grass in front of the family's new prefabricated home, north of Havant – an area that would soon grow rapidly. He fought long for this Englishman's home and was lucky to survive near drowning during the D-Day landings, when his armoured bulldozer tipped over, trapping and killing three men under it. (R. Little)

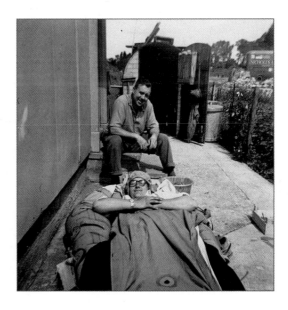

Dick and a pal take a well-earned rest outside the prefab. He said: 'I came back in rough shape. I had a blood transfusion from an American war correspondent. I was landed at Queen Alexandra Hospital and left in a corridor for hours. When my wife came down I was covered in blood and salt water and hadn't shaved.' (R. Little)

Church 'bosses' recently dictated that a 20-minute film about baptism had to be remade because it showed a woman puppet washing up and a male puppet in the 'power role' (washing the car). So what on earth would they say about this little boy playing sailors at Havant? Sorry, I couldn't find one of him playing nurses! (R. Little)

On the same subject, this one of Peter Little is even more shocking. He is indulging the male fantasy of driving a car – again at the prefabs in about 1952. (R. Little)

This was the ultimate fantasy in a bygone age — every little boy used to want to be an engine driver, so it was said. I don't know what a boy's favourite choice would be now — a girl perhaps! Reports suggest that young males are increasingly demoralized by the negative male images portrayed by the media. Dick Little built this engine for his son Peter. (R. Little)

The seeds of our modern world and all its peculiarities and contradictions were being sown when this picture was taken in Havant in 1947. Wearing her uniform as part of Britain's Peace Commission in Europe, Muriel Burrows (back row, second from left) poses with family and friends. The Commission worked toward Germany's reconstruction. I hope it is not considered offensive for me to remark that she must have added quite a bit of glamour to the proceedings. She recalls: 'I once returned home from Germany with an out-of-date ticket, but I just smiled sweetly at the ticket collector and sailed through.' (M. Hudson)

Havant Wolf Cub Scouts in the old market-place, Havant, on fund-raising duties, 19 April 1958. King John granted the town's original market charter and a market house probably stood to the east of the church, where the Homewell stream was convenient for watering animals. The market house was rebuilt several times before the market moved to its final site in Star Meadow. Old flint walls surrounded the market and there was a trough in Prince George Street where the animals took water. Eggs, fruit and flowers were sold to housewives by Mr Gates the auctioneer. War brought rationing and slowed trade. Peace and post-war socialism added a plethora of new transport and marketing rules. The market could not survive the changes and the site was sold to the North Street Arcade developers in 1957. Locals would soon be looking forward to supermarket shopping and life as a suburb of expanding Portsmouth. (*Portsmouth News*)

A far from abominable snowman with its creators, Peter Little and his Auntie Thora, December 1950. Even more to delight the lad was on the way with Santa and his sleigh bells. (R. Little)

Pony trekking on Hayling Island in the 1960s. With so much countryside around the area, it is still a popular relaxation, but can cause problems in these crowded modern times. In 1977 Havant Borough Council were asked to stop horse riders using the pedestrian area at Blackmoor Walk because they were causing problems, especially for the elderly. (M. Hudson)

The attractions of Havant's prefabs were not tempting enough to prevent this family emigrating to Australia shortly after this picture was taken in 1950. (R. Little)

Peter Little and his cousin Tony enjoying the particular pleasure of a back garden hammock. Those were the days when nature still had a chance, before fruit-machines and computer games started turning children into cyberfolk. (R. Little)

The Ford Popular car is parked in a Rowlands Castle country lane while the Little family enjoy the freedom that early post-war motoring could offer. The faces are full of hope for a brighter future. But nothing is ever perfect, not even the trusty motor car. As Dick said, 'It was the bane of my life. The wipers worked off the power of the engine, so they slowed almost to a stop when I went up hills.' (R. Little)

A family picnic in the New Forest in 1958. Cars improved rapidly during the late 1950s. Within a few years, a huge fly-over would whisk traffic off Havant's narrow streets and the 'Hayling Billy' would be no more. The country would be redesigned around the motor car so that many more people could enjoy a trip out to the New Forest and a picnic.

In spite of all the improvements, life is never plain sailing with cars, as young Peter Little found with his new 100E Ford Anglia, parked here in New Lane in about 1963. There is a view that cars enslave rather than liberate; nevertheless they are woven into our culture as something good and as a proving ground for young males. (R. Little)

As the song goes, 'I'd rather be on horseback'. This is Josie Stride at the family's smallholding near Emsworth. Those were the days when there was still some real horse power about – and with the sort of exhaust that was useful too! (M. Hill)

If you haven't got a horse then a bike is the next best thing. This is Nicola Chesterman practising her roadcraft in Elmleigh Road police station car park in about 1964. (J. Chesterman)

Nicola Chesterman was obviously well brought up, her parents ahead of their time as far as anti-sexual stereotyping is concerned. Here she is in the much-vaunted role of family car washer in about 1962. Or were her parents actually exploiting child labour? I'd better leave that to the child experts to decide! (*see* p. 60). (J. Chesterman)

At least Nicola's parents let her have a rest. It's the cat's turn to do a bit of washing! (J. Chesterman)

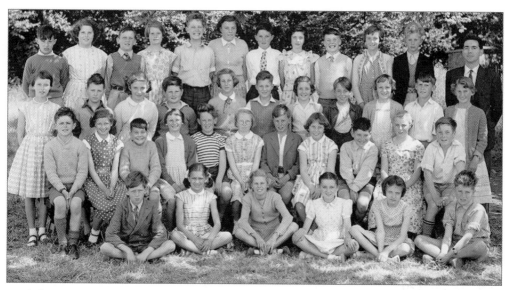

Pupils from Bosmere School in the early 1950s. Two of Jesse Hunt's children attended here, and though it was a good school it was very different from their father's experience. 'We had a lot of religious education but discipline was severe. We had no problems with bullies.' (J. Hunt)

Another tidy group from Bosmere, again in the 1950s. There were no long-haired teachers complaining about the job in those days. 'But teachers in those days weren't knee-deep in National Curriculum requirements, with all the associated form-filling, desperate to get every pupil to pass a sack-full of GCSEs in order to prove their school's brilliance. It was horses for courses in those days. Not courses for teachers' hobby horses,' said one teacher, who prefers to remain anonymous in the present sensitive educational climate! (J. Hunt)

These two photographs show pupils at Havant High School for Young Ladies, May 1965. Nicola Chesterman, fifth from left in the front row (top picture), said: 'I was very happy there. Every term we had to kneel in the dining hall and if our skirt hem was too far from the floor, our mothers had to let it down. They also checked we had name labels in our vests and knickers at the start of each term. I

remember the headmistress, Mrs Luetchford, declaiming in assembly that she'd heard a girl saying that she was sweating. She told us all that "Horses sweat, young ladies perspire." Another funny memory of mine is when they offered us piano lessons. I asked my mother to enrol me and she said, "We haven't got a piano". I said, "That's all right, you don't have to take your own".' (J. Chesterman)

Tarka, J.L. Hudson's first day boat, *c.* 1946. This was a type of airborne lifeboat which used to be dropped from Lancaster bombers for ditched aircrews. Mr Hudson was Commodore of the Yacht Club at the time of their first race from Langstone in the spring of 1946. (M. Hudson)

Mrs Muriel Hudson, née Burrows, in the garden of The Look-out, where she lived with her late husband for over forty years. The house was a regular meeting place for yacht club members. Mrs Hudson continued commuting to Civil Service work in London until the early 1970s and remembers 'there was quite a commuter club on the train'. (K. Edwards)

The ferry from Hayling to Southsea is just disappearing to the right, loaded with environmentally friendly bicycles in about 1960. (M. Hudson)

Mengham Road, South Hayling, c. 1961. These were the less sophisticated days before cool dudes and beach babes came to enjoy the surf – wind surfing was invented on Hayling. It was a good old-fashioned place to be, replete with the simple pleasures of holiday camps. South Hayling's original three settlements, West Town, Gable Head and Eastoke, are no longer so distinct, the fields between them having been inevitable targets for development over the years. William the Conqueror gave the Manor of Hayling to the Abbey of St Peter and St Mary at Jumieges, Normandy, in 1067. (M. Hudson)

Even though it is only 1963 someone seems to have told this happy group on Hayling beach about the hole developing in the ozone layer! They look very well protected! (R. Little)

Another Sunday on Hayling Beach during the early 1960s but these folk seem to be in rather more of a traditional holiday mood. There used to be a saying that if you can't afford the South of France, go to Hayling. This scene certainly looks hot enough. (R. Little)

A women's group: what else can I say without sounding controversial? Any mention of bathing beauties and I could be in trouble! It was not such a sensitive subject when this picture was taken in the early 1960s. Mary Hill is holding son Christopher. Their poodle, Nikki, performed at the local 'Chipper' pet show, riding a tricycle. I doubt that sort of thing would be allowed now either! (R. Little)

This Hayling amusement park scene looks very 1950s and the same dated charm is still there. It never needed to become commercialized to attract visitors and is still relatively unspoiled. However, there's been much growth of affluent residential areas since 1945. Former Hayling CID officer Ted Gale said: 'there were so many criminals visiting the area in the 1960s that we used to call it Treasure Island'. Working alongside colleague Tony Hill, the local crime-busters were nicknamed 'Up Hill and Down Gale'. Tony said, 'We had a tremendous success rate on Hayling because everyone knew each other and they helped us.' (V. Church)

Peter Little followed the family tradition when he built this boat. This picture was taken at Langstone in 1964. Tragically, Peter was soon stricken with leukaemia. (R. Little)

One of the Warner holiday camps that gave pleasure to thousands on Hayling Island in the 1960s. Billy Butlin started the new holiday camp craze after the Second World War, using old military camps. They were either loved or hated, and were a breeding ground for talents like Des O'Connor and Michael Barrymore. Warners owned the famous 'Hi de Hi' camp in Harwich and their head office was at Warner House, Havant. The company subsequently sold out to J. Arthur Rank, who also owned Butlins. Bill Warner continued working with the new management for a while. Ted Gale, Warner's security manager, remembers: 'We took on Henry Cooper as PR man. He was very good at shaking hands and telling us how he had knocked down Cassius Clay.' (M. Hudson)

Peace and sunshine on the walk past the Beach Club at Eastoke, Hayling Island, in the late 1950s. Detective Ted Gale remembers going to a minor burglary at Eastoke: 'This woman said her Heinz sponge pudding was missing. And just like on the adverts, this little boy screeched "Not the Heinz sponge pudding, mum?"' (M. Hudson)

Hayling Yacht Company, Mill Road, c. 1959. They were well established as builders and repairers, and their output reflects the wealth that has tempted villains on to the island over the years. Boats have always been prime targets. Ted Gale recalls responding to a tip-off and supervising the arrest of twenty-two men who had gone looking for a fight in a Northney Ballroom. Ted says, 'I always had a good rapport with villains. It was part of the job. I've had some laughs. Some of them are settled down on Hayling now. If you can't get on with the villains you're wasting your time.' (M. Hudson)

Harold Pycroft fishing Hayling waters in July 1963. The boat in the foreground is a punt, complete with 'punt gun' for shooting ducks. The Pycrofts were keen fishermen and knew all the tricks, going barefoot to check temperature differences in the water, and scrutinizing the mud and sand for signs of winkles. (Noel Pycroft)

The polite way to break wind on Hayling Island, *c.* 1960! (R. Little)

Langstone Harbour in about 1960, with the world changing around it. One local Langstone lady said, 'It was disgraceful. They emptied all the Portsmouth city dwellers into new houses at Leigh Park. These people didn't want the woods and they took fences for fires. They just wanted to go back to Portsmouth. The locals didn't want them either. Before they came you could leave all your boats and equipment on the bank at Langstone all night.'

Purbrook amateur theatre, late 1980s. The group developed out of the Brooklyn Players, started by Joy Adamson in 1967. I vividly remember my tax office section leader Mike Morley, third from the right. One of the first things I had to do in the Inland Revenue was sign the Official Secrets Act so I can't say too much! But one day I was chatting away to friends Pat and Barbara from the 'movements section' (!) when Mike came along and ordered me to go and do some expenses calculations for the Portsmouth Water Company. I did it immediately and within thirty minutes was back at my post with the 'movements' girls. Mike soon appeared behind me again and asked brusquely, 'Why aren't you doing as I asked?' 'I've done it,' I said. 'But you can't have followed the rules in that time.' 'Rules were made for the guidance of wise men and the obedience of fools,' said I. The Official Secrets Act prevents me from telling what happened next! (*Portsmouth News*)

The worst I can say about Mike is that he failed to spot a fellow thespian! Notice my intense expression while singing my favourite Neil Young song, 'Helpless', somewhere in Leigh Park in 1975. Helpless was how I felt during my Inland Revenue days! (V. Church)

My son Kieran enjoying all the fun of the Hayling fairground in 1988. For some of us simple pleasures die hard. (R. Cook)

Kieran and I skim down the Hayling helter-skelter in 1990 while son Edward wonders whether it's safe for him to have a go. The attendant of course has seen it all before and continues to improve his mind with one of the tabloids! (N. Cook)

CHANGING TIMES

Good old family values – Gwen, Dick and Peter Little,
Christmas 1964. (R. Little)

VJ-Day celebrations, Havant, 1945. At last it's all over and there's time for some fun before the little matter of putting the world back together again. It was best to make the most of it for just this one day. Freedom would not come too easily, and maybe not at all for some: the tensions of the Cold War were not far away. This was good news for the military – many jobs in the area were created during the Cold War, particularly at ASWE, Plessey and Marconi. The dockyard has suffered cutbacks since the 'success' of the Thatcher/Reagan alliance in defeating Communism in recent years. Politicians are always claiming credit for giving us more freedom, but there is always a cost. The nation has lost an Empire; Havant lost an Empire Cinema but gained the Meridian Centre. Opinions always differ when it comes to deciding whether something is a success or failure, and it seems that the most interesting thing about politicians is not their sex lives but how disasters are never their fault. Here we see simple pleasure and people full of hope. Over the years since we have seen the younger generation degenerate into a pop culture obsessed with easy pleasures, but how can they be so different from the heroic young men and women who fought for their freedom in the first place? How tragic that one generation should ever blame the other for its failures far and near. How awful that a group of Portsmouth youngsters recently dragged from his car and beat senseless an ex-Royal Marine, who was returning from a war veterans' reunion. The lessons of war were clearly not long-lasting. Is it just man's nature to be violent? Or is it just that too little thought is being given to the loss of male self-respect in a country which has abandoned so much of its old manufacturing industry in favour of services which prefer female employees. George Orwell predicted a future where ordinary men and women would be encouraged to blame each other for their miseries, while those in power pursued their interests unhindered – i.e. divide and rule. Whatever the point of view, times have certainly been changing, but hardly in the way envisaged by my old hero Bob Dylan in his idealistic song of the 1960s. (R. Little)

Dick Little at his New Lane home, reading a Sunday paper, *c.* 1960. The back page headline reads 'Six Children See the Last Grim Act'. Journalists keep delivering gruesome stories – and they sell newspapers. The violence of war was at least impersonal and pushed people together. The violence of peace does the opposite. (R. Little)

A few minutes' peace and a cuppa for Dick Little's mother at Langstone, 1959. Folk used to say a woman's work was never done and times were such that women were brought up to bear and bring up children, often helped by their own mothers. Today there are other pressures, opportunities and temptations. But all too often women end up in low paid jobs supporting their partner's income or lack of it. (R. Little)

Growing up not long after the Second World War, I saw films about war heroes and read comics about True Brits. Then I played soldiers, rather like this New Lane youngster in about 1952. Rather than wallowing in ideas of killing and aggression, I say myself as a fighter for good against evil. Now it's all too simple to conclude that playing with toy guns creates killers. The present record on youth crime is hardly an advert for the new philosophy of politically correct play. (R. Little)

J.B. Priestley wrote a book called *Men in New Suits* which dealt with hopeful young men fresh back from the Second World War and battle zones, each with a new suit and hat, thrust back into civilian life in a country nearly bankrupt. Here is Dick Little posing at Langstone in his new suit. He looks remarkably fashionable by today's standards, which just goes to show that what goes around comes around. (R. Little)

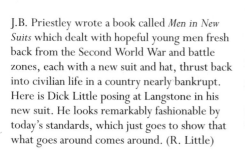

Gwen Little and her son Peter with their neighbour's children at her prefab near the Petersfield Road, north Havant, in 1948. Fifty of these prefabs were built and they were much appreciated after so many Portsmouth homes had been destroyed in the Blitz. Gwen remembers: 'All the kids were about the same age and we were surrounded by fields. It was the most enjoyable time in our lives.' (R. Little)

The prefabs soon made way for the Portsmouth overspill development of Leigh Park. Meanwhile this traditional thatched cottage at Northney, Hayling Island, has survived hundreds of years of upheaval and change. (M. Hudson)

The Wadeway, a ¾ mile long Roman trackway, was a vital link from Langstone to Hayling before the first bridge was built in 1824. The widening of Chichester Harbour in the late nineteenth century increased the tidal flow and moved the watershed at Langstone. Consequently, the rising sea level and increasing traffic necessitated a bridge. The Hayling Bridge and Causeway Company bought the 1824 bridge in 1851. It lasted until 1956, and was maintained by collecting tolls. A new bridge would have been needed sooner if the Havant–Langstone railway line had not been extended across Langstone Water as a means of getting heavier materials on and off the island. Bus conductor David Brunnen remembers trouble in the early 1950s: 'Before they built the new bridge on to Hayling passengers would have to get off the bus and walk over the bridge. We were only allowed to carry eight over on the bus. One time we were short of small coaches and borrowed some "Leyland Cheetahs" from Reading. I let eight passengers stay on as usual. When the toll-keeper saw us he had a go at me because the Reading "Cheetahs" weighed more than ours. Even the Chief Inspector got to hear about it.' But the old wooden bridge had to go and is seen here being demolished in 1956. The new bridge is higher, wider and gleaming alongside. (M. Hudson)

This picture from 1933 shows the limits of the old Langstone toll-bridge. Cynics might suspect that the London, Brighton & South Coast Railway, who took over the running of this bridge in 1851, had a vested interest in ensuring it was never improved. Efforts were made to end the tolls in 1938 and the Havant and Waterloo Urban Council became divided over the issue. Hayling folk would have to raise at least £210,000 toward the loss of revenue; this was outvoted and the tolls lasted until 1960. (*Portsmouth News*)

This 8–wheeled brick lorry was one of the first heavy vehicles to cross Langstone's new road bridge in 1956. Its driver, Jack Bromfield, was, like my father, part of the army of ex-servicemen lucky enough to get jobs delivering bricks for the London Brick Company during the years of post-war reconstruction. But everything has its price – my father died in 1962 as a result of a collapsing brick stack. The brick-making industry has always had its dangers and Jack reminded me that lorry driving was no picnic: 'The speed limit was 20 mph, there was no power steering, and with a full load the brakes were so bad that you sent a postcard to where you wanted to stop!' (J. Bromfield)

'Apres la deluge' of newcomers, motoring around Leigh Park during the early 1950s. The nation was optimistic, petrol was off ration and motorists had it all to look forward to – as yet there were no worries about the ozone layer or global warming, and the powerful motoring and oil industries had it all to look forward to as well. Portsmouth City Council bought Leigh Park in about 1946 and soon installed displaced city dwellers in this heaven. The council built the second largest housing estate in England and it was a haven for Ford Cortina and custom car enthusiasts when I lived there. So much so that I remember musing upon Middle Park Way:

> The Cortina was gleaming, he'd polished it all day,
> He knew this was the evening for fun on the highway.
> With dark of night approaching the city lights were bright,
> and a shining custom Cortina was really outasight.
> Their names were on the windscreen, in letters bold as brass,
> He'd put them up last Wednesday, said they'd add a touch of class,
> Sharon was there waiting, been ready since eight,
> she really was quite angry because her Tom was late.

Cars were the new freedom and a far cry from the days when Sir George Staunton MP was Lord of the Manor in 1820. He would never allow himself to be troubled by others: not wishing to have to wait at Bedhampton and Stockheath level-crossing, he had a new road built to link Bedhampton and Stockheath Lane. He also had the Havant to Horndean Road resited away from his mansion. (M. Hudson)

Park Parade shopping centre, *c.* 1962. Critics have said that more attention should have been paid to providing Leigh Park with proper community facilities at the outset. But Prime Minister Harold Macmillan's rather strained proclamation, 'You've never had it so good [so therefore vote for me!]' in 1959, masked Britain's economic decline. There was a rush to build the necessary homes, as cheaply as possible. It's hard to imagine a more pleasant setting for city overspill and it's easy to sensationalize Leigh Park's social problems (*see* p. 109). Also many of the first families into the Park took their problems with them and perhaps the older Havant people perceived these problems to be worse than they were. It's difficult to judge, since journalists have a tendency to exaggerate and politicians to obscure. But all appears well in this picture of hustle, bustle and sweet Saturday charm. (M. Hudson)

Jill Chesterman (right) remembers travelling to Havant from her native Cornwall, just married and aged 20: 'I arrived on a grey February day in 1957. Looking back I realize the town was on the threshold of change. In those days it was still a small market town with a cattle market at the top of North Street, small shops and very little traffic. Market Lane led to the park and its houses were soon to be demolished to make way for the new shopping centre and the first supermarket. The character of the place changed rapidly. At first I felt close to my Cornish childhood, watching potatoes being planted and then harvested in the fields opposite our house in Elmleigh Road. Those fields eventually made way for the new police station (the first police station and court house was built in 1858) and the DHSS building. I used to watch the residents of Havant collecting their benefits, some arriving and parking on our service road wearing old jeans and torn shirts, only to come back to the car and change into smart clothes and drive away for the day.' This picture shows Jill out for the day at Hayling in the early 1960s. She said: 'One of the great delights of living in Havant was the "Hayling Billy" train with its little steam engine. It travelled to and from Hayling station, depositing families on the way to the beach. There were rumours of the unsafe bridge. We held our breaths during the short time the train took to cross Langstone Harbour from Hayling to Havant, with children jumping up and down with excitement at the view of water and many boats.' (J. Chesterman)

Elmleigh Road in 1959, when Jill Chesterman noticed that: 'The traffic increased with the building of a factory estate at New Lane, and then the grammar school near the main roundabout at the end of our road. That was a road we never attempted to leave in the summer months because of the large queues of traffic coming down from London and heading for Hayling.' (J. Chesterman)

The Chestermans' new home in Elmleigh Road. This was 1950s idealism, solidly built, with character and using local bricks. Jill Chesterman remembers a near neighbouring couple had so little money left over after paying the mortgage that they took up some floorboards and dangled their legs between the joists so that the floor became a dining table. The elm trees at the top of the road (after which it was named), were felled because of Dutch Elm disease. (J. Chesterman)

Simon Chesterman, looking rather wise for a 3-year-old, riding his trike in Elmleigh Road police station car park. His Cornish mother recalls: 'When he was a baby in the pram I left him outside the butchers who were advertising real Cornish pasties. It must have been finding carrot in it when I took a bite that made me forget all about Simon. I mean you never put carrot in a proper pasty. I'd walked all the way home before I remembered the pram with Simon in it.' Still, no harm done – and Simon is now a police inspector, so he can keep his mother in order in future! (J. Chesterman)

Frank Chesterman and his grandmother-in-law Christiana ('Chrissy'). Chrissy was used to hard work and here is ready to lend a hand in building Frank's new conservatory at Elmleigh Road. Her Cornish tin-miner husband travelled as far as America seeking mining work when there was none at home. She was widowed early and had to fend for herself. Frank also travelled far, working for the Admiralty Surface Weapons Establishment (ASWE), and met his future wife at Pendeen, Cornwall, where he was conducting sea trials from the lighthouse. By way of relaxation he became an accomplished self-taught craftsman and has fond memories of Leonard Leng's antique furniture shop in Prince George Street. The bricks for his conservatory came from a brickworks at Rowlands Castle. (J. Chesterman)

Langston Sailing Club members gathering in the malt loft at the Ship Inn, Langstone. The old malt-store became The Ship pub in 1868 and the original wheel for hauling the grain is still *in situ* upstairs. Ambrose Jones and his wife Eliza raised six children in this establishment in the early days. I don't know whether they were Catholics! Many locals had large families, to cope with life's vicissitudes. But the area did have a high proportion of both Catholics and Dissenters. Since the established Church was an arm of government in those days, it was handy for such people to be near the coast for escape. Still there seem to be no dissenters among this group. Commodore J.L. Hudson, musing with his pipe, is second from the right. Members were looking forward to the club's first race in 1946 when boats with jolly names like *Nog* and *Tilly* would cut among the waves. Sidney Little is standing behind the piano; he was brought up in a cottage next to the Royal Oak. He recalls his childhood before the First World War: 'I went to school in Brockhampton Lane . . . there were twenty boys in a class and we had three teachers. They taught us everything from algebra to zoology. During the war we lost our playground to a glove factory and during breaks played safely in the road. We had gas lighting in the ceiling with two horizontal branches with naked lights at each end. The gas works was near the station.' (M. Hudson)

JUST THE TICKET

It's always the same: you wait for hours for a bus, then four come along at once. This group was photographed at Hayling Garage in 1964; they have lost their destination blinds and look ready for retirement. (A.M. Lambert)

AIX36277 Terrier Class 'Hayling Billy' engine stands with train at Hayling station, 3 May 1953. These engines weighed 28 tons 5 cwt and looked tiny next to their carriages. The railway to Hayling had been open for ninety-seven years when it closed in November 1963. It had begun by serving the needs of Langstone harbour, including a paddle steamer, *Carrier*, which took trucks to the Isle of Wight (where the old 'Hayling Billy' engine *Newington* is now working again). With lack of foresight toward tourist potential a car-mad government axed the line in 1963 because the wooden bridge was too expensive for them to fund British Railways to repair. They simply ignored the otherwise buoyant business which sold 598 tickets for one trip alone in August 1961. The line had played a vital role in developing the island's economy. The London Brighton & South Coast railway started services with four trains each way, increasing to ten by 1900. Southern Region were running seventeen in the summer of 1938 with an extra Wednesday and Saturday late service for the cinema. *The News* reported on 4 November 1963: 'Passengers joined hands and sang Auld Lang Syne in the last 'Hayling Billy' on Saturday night as it steamed with its whistle sounding continuously around the last bend to Havant station! (B.K.B. Green)

AIX32677 runs round its train in Havant, 3 May 1953. When the line closed in 1963 an ex-Blackpool tram car was purchased privately in the hope of maintaining a service. Sadly, this was not to happen. (B.K.B. Green)

AIX32677 all set for the return run to Hayling on 3 May 1953. This area of the railway became parking space for the all-conquering and polluting motor car after the line closed. The final train carried a laurel wreath on the front of the engine and *The News* reported: 'For the final trip back to Havant, to the accompaniment of detonations, whistles and cheerings from the people all along the five-mile line, the 'Billy' had its largest load ever – six coaches with Terrier tank engines at front and rear. Not only did it make a picturesque and memorable sight as it puffed busily through the moonlight, but it was also greeted by unforgettable sights all along the line.' (B.K.B. Green)

The 'unforgettable sights' greeting the last 'Hayling Billy' included people throwing open their windows, cameras flashing, people thronging fences along the line and tape recorders being used to 'catch the last familiar and distinctive sound'. It's hard to imagine the same kind of enthusiasm for buses like this which benefited from the train's demise. But looking back on the buses of the 1950s and '60s, there is much to lament about the changes bus crews have experienced over the years. This 1950s red-painted Leyland belonged to Portsmouth Corporation when it was photographed at Southdown's Emsworth garage by conductor David Brunnen. David said: 'Very often during the winter months we used to have Portsmouth Corporation buses to cover the mileage difference between the two companies. We used these vehicles on the Waterlooville–Havant–Emsworth service. One day we arrived at Bedhampton crossing and there was a lady standing there and she said to me very nicely, "were we going to Leigh Park?" I said, "No dear, you want a red one." I looked at her surprised face as we drove away and suddenly remembered we had a red bus that day! I joined Southdown in April 1954 as a trainee conductor and my family reckoned I'd last three months. That three months lasted for twenty-eight years. I had a fortnight's training and then I was let loose among the travelling public. My first week's wage was £8 9s 8d. Coming out of Portsmouth one day there was a lady on the bus with a hat with a load of hat pins in it. I caught a pin in my jacket somehow and her hat and wig came off together, much to her annoyance. The other passengers found it quite interesting!' (D. Brunnen)

Dave Brunnen was working on one of these 'Guy' open-toppers on Hayling Carnival day. 'We were coming away from Hayling ferry and the carnival pulled round out of Staunton Avenue in front of us. Then there came a gap we thought it was the end of the procession and so did the crowd which parted to let us through. The rest of the carnival was then coming up and we were in the middle, all the way from old Hayling station to Beachlands bus station. We were even getting cheered. It was smashing.' (A.M. Lambert)

A Havant-bound 'Southdown' Leyland with the added luxury of a roof and back doors, passing White's Corner, Hayling Island, 15 September 1963. Doors could be useful: Davie Brunnen recalls buses without them: 'During the 1955 rail strike I was taken off local routes and sent with double-deckers to London. We had some cases on the open platform and they all fell off into the road. We had to stop and gather them up.' (A.M. Lambert)

There was still a railway station on Hayling for this bus to call at when this picture was taken at Beachlands in September 1963. Beachlands was the centre-piece of Hayling sea front with over 100 acres of land between Sea Front Road and the shore, mostly owned by the council and preserved for public use. Picnics among the grassy dunes there, surrounded by gorse and wild flowers, have long been popular pastimes. (A.M. Lambert)

Looking almost as graceful as an ocean liner, this vintage Leyland bus is ready to set sail back from Eastoke in September 1963. But it wasn't always plain sailing on Hayling! David Brunnen remembers heading on to the island: 'On a nice spring evening I was standing on the platform watching the world go by. We weren't very busy and heard a car coming. There was a whopping great bang. This car had hit our nearside front wheel and bits of car went everywhere, canvas top and all. The driver calmly got out of the wreckage, looked at me and said, "Oh, I didn't even see the bus. My driver and I looked at each other and thought the bloke needed his eyes testing.' (A.M. Lambert)

Open-topped double-deckers were a well-established and fine way of enjoying the view on Hayling when this picture was taken outside Eastoke Café in September 1963. This view is all the better for being uncluttered by motor cars. Dave Brunnen recalls: 'The new bridge increased traffic to Hayling dramatically. One summer Sunday we picked up a bus at Havant station to go down and round Hayling and Portsmouth and back. We left Havant at 2.10 p.m. and returned at 9.45 p.m. There was consternation among the office staff concerning where on earth we'd been.' (A.M. Lambert)

I've always liked buses and here's another, again at Eastoke. Alan Lambert has captured the charm of late summer on Hayling. Young lads loiter at the bus stop and talk about what young men talk about, while a pretty girl gets ready to climb on board. The woman in the twin set and sensible shoes, clutching her handbag, completes this scene of essential English reserve and understatement. (A.M. Lambert)

An appropriately named Stagecoach bus, part of former nursing sister Anne Gloag's national bus empire, passing the former stage coach halt, The White Hart in East Street in February 1995. Before the railways this road was the busy Portsmouth–Chichester turnpike. In the 1820s stage coaches ran to Brighton, Portsmouth, Southampton and London. But so many things change. The one-man-operated bus in this picture was the last straw for David Brunnen: 'I left Southdown in April 1982. I enjoyed the work, but unfortunately the all-conquering one-man-operated bus took over; a thing which I heartily opposed right from the start. I certainly would not have worked one of those vehicles myself, especially a double-decker.' (R. Cook)

Halcyon days on Langstone Bridge in 1946. There's a proper old bus bringing up the rear of the queue. At this time the vehicle weight limit was 6 tons 6 cwt and if the specially built Leyland Cheetahs had more than eight passengers the surplus had to get out and walk across. (*Portsmouth News*)

LOOKING BOTH WAYS

A rather moth-eaten Union Jack flying over
The Look-out. Is it perhaps symbolic of a decline in
national standards? (M. Hudson)

Langston Yacht Club Commodore Les Hudson chats to a member about mooring rights between the harbour bridges in 1959. The hulk of the old gravel boat *Langstone* is visible in the centre background, almost in front of the old mill. The state and future of the harbour has been much debated and it has a past full of legend and romance. Local families such as the Littles have a solid place in the harbour's past, while the links with artists such as Flora Twort and Richard Joycie are more fragile, fleeting and chimerical. We make of artists whatever we want to. Flora Twort will no doubt be a heroine to the feminists. Her long-time friend Nevil Shute Norway is a hero to me and I always felt Langstone to be hallowed ground because he walked there. His novels blended his love of engineering with a bittersweet quest for romance. He must have found Langstone harbour stimulating during his sojourns with Flora. He also organized part of his aircraft production company in a shed behind Langstone Towers, which were used as a First World War hospital. But the Second World War was the great watershed, much greater than the one between Chichester and Langstone; the rate at which the old ways were eroded by the tide of change was fast. Nevil Shute captured it all in his novels and left for Australia while England withered under a weight of urban growth. Langstone felt the effects of increased sewage discharges and seaweed growth sparked an environmentalist to campaign for a clean-up in 1976. But Havant Borough Council saw the expense of a clean-up as a threat to its housing programme – especially the £25 million 1,400-unit estate at Stakes Hill Lodge Estate, Waterlooville. Fortunately the County Council supported plans to make Langstone a conservation area, but with continued population growth the pressure on the harbour's natural environment will increase. (M. Hudson)

One of the two faces of Langstone, photographed by resident Kevin Edwards. Here the sun is setting and all is calm. . . .

But beware the smile on the face of the tiger, it can change at any moment. A storm is up over Langstone. On such occasions there was a great danger of flooding in the Royal Oak's cellar – this often brought the cry 'get the beer up'. (K. Edwards)

'Hello, hello, hello, what's all this then?' It's PC Tony Hill of Havant, and as they say, when policemen look that young you know you are getting old. Tony said: 'In my early days with Portsmouth police we had to prove we were doing the job by getting some names in the notebook. I've booked cyclists for not stopping at road junctions. There were lots of them!' There still are, and given that road deaths vastly outnumber murders and violent assaults it's a pity that traffic policing does not have a higher status in the force. (A.C. Hill)

To some people police cars have a touch of glamour, but it's the murder squad that captures the imagination of TV script writers. This picture pre-dates all that nonsense. Cadets Hill (left) and Oakshot pose beside a gleaming 2½-litre Riley squad car at Portsmouth HQ in 1952. Tony has learned a lot about life during his police career. One of the grimmest events concerned the death of Larry King in Havant thicket, between Leigh Park and Rowlands Castle. Tony explained: 'The Leigh Park gangs were active in Havant during the late 1960s. They could reach through the letterbox of Ryan's ironmongers and get axes off the display stand. They also raided beer barrels behind The Star pub. One day they stole a scooter and took it into Havant thicket for a bit of fun. When it ran out of petrol Larry attacked it with an axe. One of them must have said "That's no way to treat a scooter" and hacked him to death.' The rest of the story is even more macabre. Walkers found a hole dug in the undergrowth of Rowlands Castle woods. It looked like a grave and so the police were called. Tony said: 'We camped out there for days to see if anyone came to bury a body. We didn't know about the King murder then. A jogger got a bit of a shock when we dived out of our bivouacs to arrest him. Eventually we gave up. Then, some days later, someone walking a dog discovered a hand poking up out of the ground in Havant thicket and it turned out to be the badly decomposed body of Larry King in a shallow grave. One of the killers ran away to sea and confessed while he was in port in South Africa. He named the other one and I posed as a prisoner in the cells between them in Havant, so that I could listen to the conversation between them.' (A.C. Hill)

This 1995 view across Havant Park contrasts the 1960s ideal of Park Parade with the Meridian complex of the 1990s. I can remember looking across from a tax office window at this view during the rainy season of March 1975, recalling more romantic moments out there in the sunshine, holding hands and all that silly stuff. The park was rainswept and dreary, and I was suffering from an overdose of tax returns. There was never any shortage of paper in the tax office and so I found a bit and started to write:

'Rain in the park'

Rain is a place on the map inside my time,
where it's always wet and windy and the leaves are green and fine,
where I sit and count the footsteps that fall upon the street,
mumble through the darkness and walk upon my feet.
To walk on feet forever, making footprints in the dark,
where one can't see the ugly for the rain inside the park.
In this place I walk forever, learning things I'll never know,
giving sorrow to the sad ones and music to the show.
But it's only sounds they're hearing, not feelings I can give,
I'm sad because I'm lonely and can't show them how to live.
So many people know how to buy and sell a friend,
but these things are much too precious for me to even lend.
If only I could teach her what I'd really meant to say
then she'd know how much I'd loved her and forget to go away.

Maybe my lines make no sense, like lots of things. (V. Church)

The last members of a long line of the Pycroft brickmaking family busy at their works on Hayling Island during the early 1970s. Unlike Fletton brickmaking (see pp. 36 and 89) they took brick earth from a few feet below the surface and worked it into a paste called pug. It was much softer than the Fletton clay and was forced into teak moulds rather than undergoing the powerful pressing process of Flettons. Also there was no carbon within the clay to make it burn like Fletton clay. Therefore the whole process was much more time-consuming and expensive, but resulted in a much better brick. The Pycrofts used to make 500 bricks an hour – Noel said it was 600 before his wife reached her 40th birthday! Six separate moulds were used with the machine shown in this picture. (N. Pycroft)

Noel Pycroft's daughter-in-law learning the trade in what was very much a family business. She is moulding bricks in about 1973. (N. Pycroft)

Christopher Pycroft working barefoot, as was the family custom, in this early 1970s picture. He is shovelling clay into the tiny hopper wagon on their homemade railway. The family made most of their tools and wasted little. The rails in this picture came from Hipkins brewery, Emsworth, where they carried grain. Noel's father Harold bought them in 1934. The Pycroft routine was to lay out their equipment in May and start brickmaking in June. Part-timers would swell the tiny labour force during school holidays. During his final days of brickmaking in 1989, Noel said: 'The college boys are remarkable. They keep interested in what they are doing and at 16 are very hard workers. Don't decry the youth of today – the ones we get are great.' (N. Pycroft)

Noel Pycroft working on a 'hack' in 1989. This is where the clay bricks were left to dry. Noel used to set them with the first course aligned south-west to north-east to make the best of the prevailing winds, and when they were dry enough the bricks were 'skintled', turned to aid even drying. The little pitch roofs in the picture were there to keep the rain and direct sunlight off the bricks and were called 'loos'. Drying took around ten days. This old way of brickmaking is still popular with seekers of quality but too expensive for large-scale housing developments. (N. Pycroft)

The Pycroft family began making bricks on the corner of Euston Road and Velder Avenue, Portsmouth, in 1887, using material from a layer of brick earth about 3 ft below the surface, which stretched from Southampton to Brighton. On Hayling Island Noel conserved his own resources and gathered material from building sites or wherever he could find it. His wife said: 'It was the story of my life, finding clay and ash from rubbish tips. We used the ash to burn the bricks. If we were out driving and saw a lorry loaded with clay we'd chase after it. In this picture Noel and his grandson barrow ash to burn a new set of bricks. (N. Pycroft)

This is one of the last pictures of the Pycrofts' brickworks on Hayling, before Noel's retirement in 1991. The 'hacks' are in the foreground and far left is the clamp where as many as 70,000 bricks were stacked for firing (baking). Stacking is an art gained from experience. Bottom layers of partially fired bricks from an earlier clamp are arranged to allow free passage of air. The fire gets up to 1,500°C and then the bricks start to burn themselves. Noel recalls: 'My great-grandfather William Pycroft built a clamp at St Mary's Road, Portsmouth, of 1,700,000 bricks in about 1862. He was the first Pycroft to make bricks and married a Portsmouth brickmaker Emma Dopson and so the family came to Hayling in 1901.' (N. Pycroft)

Belmont Tavern, early 1960s. Built close to Belmont Park Lodge gates, it was demolished to make way for housing which extended into neighbouring park and farmland as the borough continued to expand. The local landscape has been ever changing and nearly two thousand years of history has been largely obscured by later development.

St Faith's Church at Havant crossroads is one of the few remaining signposts to the past and is shown here in about 1960. This crossroads was built over ancient Roman tracks which ran from Bitterne to Chichester, along the south coast road from Winchester, through Rowlands Castle to Langstone. The crossing was made here because of the Homewell stream which never dried out in winter. (M. Hudson)

The White Hart in East Street. This pub was rebuilt when North Street was widened in 1889. The Duke of Norfolk repaired here for refreshment in 1824, before opening Hayling bridge. In later years so did many of my old tax office colleagues, celebrating an excellent turnover of monthly post. I never went with them, but often called alone to drink. I recall some interesting clientele during the mid-'70s. In those days I had an unhealthy appetite for Guinness and cigarettes, which my salary was hard-pressed to meet. One Tuesday evening I was perched upon a bar stool, all tight blue jeans and blonde curly hair, when I was approached by a middle-aged man called Les. Naivety written all over my face, I accepted free pints galore and enough cigarettes to make me dizzy. Speaking with a Yorkshire accent, Les explained that he was a merchant seaman. While we talked a number of his friends and fellow sailors joined us. 'Would you like to have dinner with me?' I thought I heard him say above the increasing hum of voices, while I was preoccupied scanning the horizon for more uplifting female company, and as I watched a girl approach I failed to answer him. He must have noticed because I heard him say: 'I don't like gales'. Allowing for the accent, I thought he meant girls and slipped off my stool in alarm. He must have guessed he'd blown it and quickly corrected it to 'Gales, Gales Ale, I don't like Gales Ale.' Which was odd because he'd been drinking it all night. I daresay this old coach house has heard better stories over the years but that's the best I can remember. (R. Cook)

Land Army milkmaids demonstrate their worth at Bedhampton. Changing roles for women was one major result of the two World Wars. But feminist demands are still not satisfied. There was a time when women issued white feathers to men who would not face the carnage of battlefields. But now all that's forgotten and men are supposed to be less assertive. Evidence suggests that many young men are confused about their role in society. Middle-aged ladies used to pat my bottom in the tax office but nowadays if that happens to a girl it's a serious matter. How attitudes change. (*Portsmouth News*)

Langstone Mill. I remember looking across at this from the Royal Oak next door, while drinking with tax office girlfriends. It was the only time I ever saw Richard Joicey, back in my 1970s heyday. He was loading his dinghy. Jill, a lively Midlander, wolf-whistled at his bronzed and muscular body. Much to my alarm, Joicey chugged up to the quay in his boat and threatened to punch me on the nose, which wasn't really fair considering that I can hardly whistle. But the story says a bit about stereotyping. (K. Edwards)

Daisy the flower seller has watched the ebb and flow of life in West Street for nearly thirty years and seen the latest changes. Almost timeless herself, here she is standing near St Faith's Church in March 1996. (R. Cook)

Inside the Meridian Centre. Is this cool or cold? Long-time councillor and author Ralph Cousins (*see Bygone Havant*) said: 'Considering what the old arcade was like, I don't think we lost anything worth keeping. Ask people if they'd want to swap it back . . . I think they'd say no.' (R. Cook)

A lone shopper walks between a vacant shop unit which bears the optimistic mural of the SS *Meridian* about to be launched by a champagne bottle, and the Noddy car. Britain has gone retail mad and there are many out of town shopping facilities. One outraged local said: 'The Meridian must be the most expensive walkway in Britain. And we've lost all those lovely little specialist shops. They used to offer something different.' (R. Cook)

But you can't stop what the mighty and their followers call progress. Here the information superhighways Nynex cable is being laid. Some might say this is the greatest concept in world history, and the more people sitting behind VDUs and clicking away with their mouses, gazing bleary-eyed at terminals, the faster our progress; the better we will all understand our role and our place. But wherever there is order there will always be irritating sceptics like me! (K. Edwards)

Marriage used to be the bedrock of society. This is a reassuring scene, the wedding of Mary Stride and Tony Hill at Bedhampton Church in June 1952. Even now we need a little romance, but how does that reconcile with the world of careers? Women want so much more and why shouldn't they? But one out of three marriages ends in divorce and men are now often the losers. It used to be the women who had to put up with every misery a bad man had to offer. (R. Little)

Veteran photographer Michael Edwards outside his Havant studio. He has photographed a few weddings in his time, as well as other local happenings. On this occasion he was the 'victim' and he had these words of advice for the photographer, his son Kevin: 'I don't know why you're bothering, you've got no depth of field, the lights's bad and it won't come out.'

This train is definitely looking both ways, but at first sight is deceptively modern, like today's electrical multiple units (EMUs), now common on the line. But this is actually an M-class loco, number 30110, sandwiched between a special train of carriages on 3 May 1953. There were plans to upgrade the Hayling line and use these heavier M7s. But with typical lack of foresight the government preferred closure – interestingly the Minister of Transport at the time was Ernest Marples, a member of the Marples Ridgeway road-building concern. (B.K.B. Green)

I photographed this old British motorbike combo in front of the old Congregational (now United Reform) Church in Havant in May 1996. It was nice to hear and see this sleepy old piece of British craftsmanship's heart beating along the old North Street. The old ways have not all gone it seems. The church dates back to 1891 and changed names following a merger with the Presbyterian Church. (R. Cook)

Nature's ways will win in the end, however much people choose to bury their heads in the sand, but coastal erosion *can* be held at bay. Mechanically loading up dredgers with shingle is a contentious business, as we see here on Hayling in 1990. Former sailor George Becconsall, now living on South Hayling, told *The News* in March 1974: 'It is my opinion that our beaches are slowly but surely finding their way into the holds of various dredgers which are operating sometimes 24 hours a day. The beach is disappearing pebble by pebble and the sea is coming ever closer.' (R. Little)

Part of the old Roman Wadeway at Langstone, close to the home of the late Les Hudson. Les described himself as 'just a man interested in nature'. He told *The News* (March 1974) that he had seen many changes in the coastline and was surprised to discover that 'where the fiercest dredging has gone on over the years, one tends to find the least change'. He remembers watching dredgers on the Hayling side of Langstone harbour since 1919 and thought that the shingle removed was simply replaced by the next wave. (M. Hudson)

My fondest memory of new industry in Havant is of the smart IBM people in their immaculate suits, proudly displaying company badges on their lapels while they took pub lunches in local pubs. They always stood out in the crowd for pub grub. The area always welcomed new industry, from as far back as the 1930s when plane maker Nevil Shute Norway observed that 'Portsmouth had everything to offer us. Had the great Commonwealth flying boat terminal been built at Langstone, Havant would have been engulfed in Portsmouth's prosperity sooner.' But it had to wait for the post-war period and a succession of plans to expand the population in the south-east. Working for the Inland Revenue familiarized me with new types of industry, including the ex-railway porter who went on to develop Hayling Marina before plunging into bankruptcy. As an electric guitar enthusiast, Goodmans Loudspeakers were my favourite. This picture shows the company's cabinet room in the late 1980s. Goodmans was founded as a family firm in the 1930s, and is now the largest UK producer of loudspeakers, selling to eighty-four countries. Their latest 155,000 sq. ft factory at the Ridgeway Centre, Havant, is a far cry from their original Axiom Works in Wembley. Production was originally in Downley Road but the new consolidated works has outstanding facilities, including an anechoic test chamber to provide acoustic measurements to the highest degree of accuracy. Other interesting Havant manufacturers include Fred Francis mini models which started in New Lane in 1954. Francis made Scalextric models and were taken over by Lines Bros. Profitability dictated that the business transferred to Kent in 1970. (Goodmans Loudspeakers)

Profit consideration is now the ultimate master. These council houses on the edge of Leigh Park look altogether more substantial than the flat tops of Sandleford Road (*see* p. 13), and the surrounding woodland looks idyllic. But space and resources were running out by the 1970s and the old ideals would fade and die in the Thatcher era. On 14 January 1975 *Portsmouth News* reported: 'A 3-bedroom house in the Havant Borough is now making a weekly loss for the council of up to £26 per week.' The council was forced to keep each property rent at £7 a week, leading to a total loss of £60,000 per year on two thousand-plus properties. (M. Hudson)

Local butcher Freddie Vine looking larger than life. Showmanship has long been part of the butchery trade: A notice in Standings window during the 1930s read 'Sausages from pigs that died happy'. (K. Edwards)

Many tenants opted for Thatcher's 'Right to Buy' policy and so took a stake in the property-owning democracy. For the less well off it was not so easy and homelessness increased. These flats on Leigh Park are one of the cheapest solutions to the problem and arguably are an improvement on the fifty prefabs built near here in 1947. (R. Cook)

Looking like a cathedral to the religion of a throwaway age, Havant incinerator just won't give up smoking. But the end of this particular faith is near. Twenty years ago this was thought to be a safe way to dispose of the daily dirt and rubbish. But researchers gnawed away at official confidence and complacency, the cancer links to the dioxin outpourings became ever more certain and the plant will soon be decommissioned. This view is from the old IBM car park, an area which was once Ann Watts' forty acre pasture. (R. Cook)

Local businessman Kevin Edwards with MP David Willetts; both are men of the 1990s and hold strong views on Havant's future. Willetts may be a long-term candidate for Tory party leader. As a public service minister with a direct line to John Major, he has proposed a plan to make single women available for work when their children reach the age of five. There are a million lone parents receiving benefits – half of them have never married. (Julian Brightwell)

A family gathering at Langstone in 1944. John Major has made much of the need for a return to 'family values', but can such things, whatever they are or were, be reconstructed in our profit-motivated, throwaway society? (R. Little)

ACKNOWLEDGEMENTS

Many people helped me to assemble this book. There is not room here to explain all their various contributions but I hope that I have done them justice. They are listed below in alphabetical order. Special thanks to my old friend and former colleague Muriel Hudson and to Mary and Tony Hill who pointed me in some good directions. All reasonable efforts have been made to trace photographic copyright holders. I am very grateful to the *Portsmouth News* for permission to reproduce from their collection and to quote from their pages.

Julian Brightwell • Jack Bromfield • David Brunnen • Ruth Brunnen • Geoff Burrows
Frank Chesterman • Jill Chesterman • Sylvia Church • Vernon Church • Nicola Cook
Ralph Cousins • David Dew • Kevin Edwards • Dave Evans • Ted Gale
Goodmans Loudspeakers • B.K.B. Green • Thor Halley • A.O. Hill • M.J. Hill
J.M. Howard • Muriel Hudson • Jess Hunt • Alan Lambert • Dick Little • Gwen Little
Judy Ounsworth • *Portsmouth News* • Portsmouth Hospitals, • Mr and Mrs Noel Pycroft

Finally, thanks also go to my wife and her family who knew Havant so much better than me.

BRITAIN IN OLD PHOTOGRAPHS

berystwyth & North Ceredigion
round Abingdon
cton
lderney: A Second Selection
long the Avon from Stratford to
  Tewkesbury
ltrincham
mersham
round Amesbury
nglesey
rnold & Bestwood
rnold & Bestwood: A Second
  Selection
rundel & the Arun Valley
shbourne
round Ashby-de-la-Zouch
ro Aircraft
ylesbury
alham & Tooting
anburyshire
arnes, Mortlake & Sheen
arnsley
ath
eaconsfield
edford
edfordshire at Work
edworth
everley
exley
deford
lston
rmingham Railways
shop's Stortford &
  Sawbridgeworth
shopstone & Seaford
shopstone & Seaford: A Second
  Selection
ack Country Aviation
ack Country Railways
ack Country Road Transport
ackburn
ackpool
round Blandford Forum
etchley
olton
ournemouth
adford
aintree & Bocking at Work
recon
rentwood
ridgwater & the River Parrett
idlington
ridport & the Bride Valley
rierley Hill
ighton & Hove
ighton & Hove: A Second
  Selection
ristol
round Bristol
rixton & Norwood
arly Broadstairs & St Peters
omley, Keston & Hayes

Buckingham & District
Burford
Bury
Bushbury
Camberwell
Cambridge
Cannock Yesterday & Today
Canterbury: A Second Selection
Castle Combe to Malmesbury
Chadwell Heath
Chard & Ilminster
Chatham Dockyard
Chatham & Gillingham
Cheadle
Cheam & Belmont
Chelmsford
Cheltenham: A Second Selection
Cheltenham at War
Cheltenham in the 1950s
Chepstow & the River Wye
Chesham Yesterday & Today
Cheshire Railways
Chester
Chippenham & Lacock
Chiswick
Chorley & District
Cirencester
Around Cirencester
Clacton-on-Sea
Around Clitheroe
Clwyd Railways
Clydesdale
Colchester
Colchester 1940–70
Colyton & Seaton
The Cornish Coast
Corsham & Box
The North Cotswolds
Coventry: A Second Selection
Around Coventry
Cowes & East Cowes
Crawley New Town
Around Crawley
Crewkerne & the Ham Stone
  Villages
Cromer
Croydon
Crystal Palace, Penge & Anerley
Darlington
Darlington: A Second Selection
Dawlish & Teignmouth
Deal
Derby
Around Devizes
Devon Aerodromes
East Devon at War
Around Didcot & the Hagbournes
Dorchester
Douglas
Dumfries
Dundee at Work
Durham People

Durham at Work
Ealing & Northfields
East Grinstead
East Ham
Eastbourne
Elgin
Eltham
Ely
Enfield
Around Epsom
Esher
Evesham to Bredon
Exeter
Exmouth & Budleigh Salterton
Fairey Aircraft
Falmouth
Farnborough
Farnham: A Second Selection
Fleetwood
Folkestone: A Second Selection
Folkestone: A Third Selection
The Forest of Dean
Frome
Fulham
Galashiels
Garsington
Around Garstang
Around Gillingham
Gloucester
Gloucester: from the Walwin
  Collection
North Gloucestershire at War
South Gloucestershire at War
Gosport
Goudhurst to Tenterden
Grantham
Gravesend
Around Gravesham
Around Grays
Great Yarmouth
Great Yarmouth: A Second
  Selection
Greenwich & Woolwich
Grimsby
Around Grimsby
Grimsby Docks
Gwynedd Railways
Hackney: A Second Selection
Hackney: A Third Selection
From Haldon to Mid-Dartmoor
Hammersmith & Shepherds Bush
Hampstead to Primrose Hill
Harrow & Pinner
Hastings
Hastings: A Second Selection
Haverfordwest
Hayes & West Drayton
Around Haywards Heath
Around Heathfield
Around Heathfield: A Second
  Selection
Around Helston

Around Henley-on-Thames
Herefordshire
Herne Bay
Heywood
The High Weald
The High Weald: A Second
  Selection
Around Highworth
Around Highworth & Faringdon
Hitchin
Holderness
Honiton & the Otter Valley
Horsham & District
Houghton-le-Spring &
  Hetton-le-Hole
Houghton-le-Spring & Hetton-le-
  Hole: A Second Selection
Huddersfield: A Second Selection
Huddersfield: A Third Selection
Ilford
Ilfracombe
Ipswich: A Second Selection
Islington
Jersey: A Third Selection
Kendal
Kensington & Chelsea
East Kent at War
Keswick & the Central Lakes
Around Keynsham & Saltford
The Changing Face of Keynsham
Kingsbridge
Kingston
Kinver
Kirkby & District
Kirkby Lonsdale
Around Kirkham
Knowle & Dorridge
The Lake Counties at Work
Lancashire
The Lancashire Coast
Lancashire North of the Sands
Lancashire Railways
East Lancashire at War
Around Lancaster
Lancing & Sompting
Around Leamington Spa
Around Leamington Spa:
  A Second Selection
Leeds in the News
Leeds Road & Rail
Around Leek
Leicester
The Changing Face of Leicester
Leicester at Work
Leicestershire People
Around Leighton Buzzard &
  Linslade
Letchworth
Lewes
Lewisham & Deptford:
  A Second Selection
Lichfield